The
Burnt
Pages

The Burnt Pages

POEMS BY

John Ash

RANDOM HOUSE

NEW YORK

Originally published in Great Britain by Carcanet Press Ltd., Manchester.

Some of the poems in this book were originally published
in *Bête Noire, Boulevard, Conjunctions, Mudfish,*
The New Yorker, O-blek, The Paris Review, and *P. N. Review.*

Library of Congress Cataloging-in-Publication Data

Ash, John.
    The burnt pages : poems / by John Ash. — 1st ed.
      p.   cm.
    ISBN 0-679-40175-X
    I. Title.
    PR6051.S37B87   1991   821'.914—dc20   90-53469

Manufactured in the United States of America
98765432
First U.S. Edition
Book design by Jo Anne Metsch
The text of this book was set in Galliard.

Contents

The
Burnt
Pages

In Rainy Country

It was already the landscape of the past,
streaked with illusionary colours—
all of it displaced, tilted at a crazy angle,
blazing with the rare sunlight of a rainy country,
all of it impossible though it was only the place
where you had lived for too many years—

all of it *below, behind,*
the tamed river curling out of the burnt blue hills
crossed by the massive red arches of a viaduct
(and none of it to be seen again, except through fog),
the city bristling and blurring as it sank away,
knowing it had failed like Ephesus,
a port the great ships no longer visited, a place to leave.

The world was an aureole
surrounding a small, sealed window,
and you turned from the glass astonished and in tears
at the start of a new trajectory.

The air was so sweet
on your arrival it was as if
the trees in the park blossomed, although the year was ending,
ending in glory. You had crossed the ocean. Now
you stepped from the avenue into the rotunda
and smiled toward the statue of a woman. Wine was poured
at the top of the curving stairs and the mirrors
were filled with the faces of those who justified
all your waiting, messengers from another life.
Each one arrived with a nimbus, each smile sang
of an understanding that would last beyond
    the framing curtains of this night.

There would be multiplications and extensions,
polyphonic variations on the deathless theme, which now
you held in your hand like a brilliant maple leaf
salvaged from the ruin of a noble valley.

So if the cold abraded your ears,
or if your coattails blew about in the merciless
wind of Seventh Avenue, it did not matter;
you were on your way to purchase music or help love prosper.

What is left behind is irretrievable,
but continues like a melody
whose logical and grieving progression nothing can halt.

Impossible not to think of it now—
the horror that fell on my father like a wolf and nearly tore him
    out of life.
And Mother? Mother suffers more quietly,
a weeping scale on a piano, and the piano distant.

Forgetting

I lived in suburbs so long,
I may never get over it. Yet those days
are obscure as the details of a drunken stupor,
in which, perhaps, you denounced enemies
or declared your love, while mist and the enamel
of moonlight settled in the empty canal.

Where were the grocery stores
when you needed them at three in the morning?
Where was the sense of immediate association
with people who just happened to be
in great numbers on the same street as you?

The world's largest and most vulgar cathedral
rises on your right; on your left the forecourt
of a mausoleum is overgrown with grass.

Who's dead in there?
you wonder, and why is it always
impossible to take home all the flowers
you saw in the florist's: not just the purple tulips,
the yellow tulips, and lilies spotted with blood,
but all the flowers whose names
you never had the patience to learn?

I know I mix the present with the past,
but that's how I like it:
there is no other way to go on.

The bungalows drift off indifferently
and sink in the reservoir. Only
the carefully tended rose beds remain
floating on the surface. The uneven steps descend

through young willows and sprouting weeds
to absolute mud and rushes—
origin of this ignominious kingdom—
and the unprofitable sunsets are shut down.

Once, under that signature of light,
we lived in the dream of a past that never existed
except in the ogival arches
and Ionic capitals of doorways painted white.
Now a strong leader has come amongst us,
and, in consequence, we know nothing.

The future is a locked factory gate.
Leaves cling in thousands to the chain-link fences,
but the trees that once stood, bigger than clouds,
overshadowing all the houses I lived in
are cut down. I remember
glowing, unlit candles, and some kind
of polished wooden jewels kids in cemeteries
collected in conditions close to ecstasy
(they vanished long ago, folded
into a thick cloak of years).

The sky above the roof was crazy with swallows.
We looked out of slits smaller than our eyes
to see the lilac die or the pear tree break into flames.

Prelude to Mammon

When the autumn came they ran
to the opera to applaud the horses.

Star-systems suspended
from their drooping shoulders, they complained
that the slaves were the wrong colour.
The children were grave, the horses black and plumed.

The sky was like the lining of a dome
in Ravenna, the sunlight an arrow.

On solitary evenings when
the pavements glistened
they snarled and paced in the shadow
of dark armoires, or giant buildings
resembling them. Students of metamorphosis,

they knew the question was not
when the new book or film or concerto
would be finished, but when it could be
abandoned. They loved the empty spaces

like perfect fields of purple loosestrife
in which planets might appear
in the torn shifts of extinct mythologies,
and perhaps favour them with a word or phrase:
"Not now. Not yet. Perfidious.
Mask of bone that once gave song."

Uncertainty

Monteverdi is already forgotten and the scene is dark though not oppressively so. Perhaps "handsomely subdued" would be the best way to describe it. The sun appears to be setting in a pronounced declivity that interrupts a distant line of misty hills (where blue-green mingles with silver and charcoal). Alternatively the sun might be rising, since there is no way of knowing whether we are looking east or west. The whole composition is arranged along an implied diagonal running from lower left to upper right. At lower left is a group of richly dressed baroque gentlemen. At upper right a huge, very pale planetary disk, obviously carved out of ivory, floats on a background of turbulent, faintly illumined cloud, coloured like dark metals. The disk would appear to be the moon (since the sun is setting or rising behind it) but a moon of a size and distinctness rarely, if ever, seen. What kind of night is this? Italian and Luna-tick . . .

The baroque gentlemen are three in number. One of them (who is standing and is closest to the picture's edge) is wearing a bright crimson cap. His face is in profile and inclined downward. He is otherwise obscure. Below him a young man is half-lying on the ground in an elegant, even epicene posture, supporting himself on one arm and with the other seeming to shield his face from the too-powerful rays of the moon (if indeed it is the moon). He is wearing a padded, narrow-waisted costume that is the same tawny orange as the sunset. He is a dandy of sorts, or perhaps only a good-looking young man with the usual vanity and pretensions, but however this may be, it is the third man who is most crucial to the moment captured here. It is he who is the chief actor in this immobile drama. He is dressed in gold and a deep midnight blue. A cloak of the latter colour is gathered about his waist in some manner. His left, yellow-clad leg is bent at the knee and his left foot rests decisively on the largest of a number of small boulders scattered on the ground before him. He is holding a block or book of the same deep blue that he is wearing, on which is inscribed a gold image of the planetary disk. Or perhaps the block or book is a mirror of some kind (a reducing mirror) and the image is a reflection. He seems to be displaying the image to its original as if expecting some sign of approval.

Standing in front of the gentlemen, and clearly the focus of their attentions (the reason for their being out in wild country so early or so late), is a tall contrivance that is probably a telescope, or just possibly some kind of device for measuring angles (the angles and distances of stars). A metal pole (I assume it to be metal—it has that gleam) rises from an elaborate base divided into three main tiers. The lowest of these is a kind of concave-sided pyramid that resolves itself into a short cylinder that supports the second tier—a broad, horizontal disk, somewhat like a café table, bordered by drooping ropes or swags. Above this is a form resembling a tightly closed tulip or lily from which the pole—an exaggerated pistil— protrudes. Fixed to the pole at an angle of about 45 degrees, and a little more than halfway up, is the telescope itself. (Yes, we have decided it is, indeed, a telescope.) It is this angle (this burnished line) that links men and moon.

Clearly these are three enlightened noblemen (or conceivably two enlightened noblemen and a servant employed by one of the two) who have ventured out at evening to investigate the mysteries of the cosmos, and we must applaud their endeavour for certainly it would have been easier for them to stay at home in their palaces, surrounded by frescoes glorifying the innumerable members of their families (here is Mother illumined by a sunburst, and here is Grandfather in the guise of Zeus), and yet there is something they have missed, for nothing could be more mysterious than the landscape in which they appear so easily ensconsed, with its raised fan of five feathery trees, its retreating series of dim, steplike cataracts, its foreground plunged in ruddy shadow.

The Strategikon *or*
Don't Go Out of the Door

Since he came from an old and noble family,
we may assume that General Cecaumenus
wanted for nothing. There were wines in his cellars,
sweetmeats at his table; on the walls of his chambers
Samson and Achilles, David and Alexander
performed their heroic exploits in stucco and paint,
and beyond the doors of his mansion the manifold
delights of the greatest city of that time
were spread out as if for a banquet: the wharves
were crowded with ships; under the colonnades
the shops were stocked with finely crafted
enamels, ivories and silks;
solemn music sounded from the churches,
and the portals of the Sacred Palace, and through
the crowds of Latins, Persians, Jews and Greeks
the great ladies, in the afternoon, hurried home,
accompanied by slaves and clouds of rare perfume,
for an evening of recitations from the Classics
or the latest erotic novels. Yet these are the words
that General Cecaumenus, in his wisdom, saw fit
to set down in his famous *Strategikon:*
"Never let a friend reside for long in your home,
for he may seduce your wife. Rather let him
lodge elsewhere, and send him the necessary food.
Secure your daughters as if they were criminals.
Avoid all parties. In sum, unless you are about
the emperor's business stay at home with your most
trusted servants, and hoard supplies against emergencies.
Only in this way can a wise man hope to avoid evil."

Three Poems

1.

It must be a quiet night. The TV announcer informs us of an old scandal concerning a Roman site near Manchester, England. (Shots of foundations, potsherds, a brick arch, a nearby parking lot, and the Palladian offices of lawyers.) It seems that sometime in 1945 certain valuable artifacts were stolen from the site, and, until now, the culprits were thought to be GIs stationed nearby, with time on their hands, and an interest in history and commerce. How else to explain the puzzling appearance of a bronze mirror, a tear bottle, a battered inscription of the time of Hadrian, and a rare coin of King Menander in Des Moines? But today it is reliably reported that the theft was executed by John Ash, a poet currently residing in New York City. It is—it goes without saying—useless to protest that the event occurred some three years before my birth. In the Protestant nations guilt is not something earned or acquired. It is, like the wealth of princes, something you are born to—a mansion, or estate, a blunt tower on 5th. It is, indeed, a peaceful night, mild and wet as a night in Manchester, under the massive porch of the Central Library.

2.

A boy and a girl are walking beside a forest. The light is slowly fading. Birds call their last notes and harmless insects hover in clouds. She tells him that his lies and pretences are apparent to everyone. He is destroying what is left of their family's standing by claiming to be a guest of the V. family, whereas it is universally known that they are staying here, on the outer perimeter of this fashionable resort, purely on the sufferance of the B. family—vulgar, bourgeois persons of no consequence—who can barely afford the rent on their dim and cluttered summer home, with its pianola and floral washstands: "Oh the songs that they play and we, remember, must sleep in that suffocating attic." She adds, "In future, please don't make things worse for us." She is older than he, and understanding has embittered her. Their feet crush the flowers of wild garlic. He only remembers a peacock's opened fan, and an avenue of trees that seemed to climb to heaven, but does not know where these things might have been. She picks a long stem of cow parsley and waves it about her head to ward off flies, and, since it is impossible for them to be at odds for very long, they join hands and set off along the path through the forest. It grows dark. There are briars and fungi. The moon rises like a Roman coin. At a short distance a lighted veranda awaits them. Tonight they will sing with the rest of the family, and the big black stupid dog (its coat full of burrs) will love them once again. White flowers glimmer at the borders of the path. They will not lose their way. It is the end of summer in Sweden, perhaps, or Russia in another century.

3 .

Eminent Excellencies, I am not a member of the families of Ducas, Dalassenus or Comnenus. Still less do I belong to the tribes of the Palaeologi or the Cantacuzeni. About the families of Phocas, Sclerus or Bardas I know next to nothing. Nor am I closely related to the houses of Angelus, Vatatzes, Lascaris or Murtzuphlus. The Botaneites, Metochiotes and the Lecapeni I hold in the lowest esteem. Nor am I a Bryennius, and the Nicephoritzes fill me with disgust. Similarly the families Apocaucus and Contopaganus. I did not know Leichudes when he rose to the Patriarchate. Nor am I a Caucumen, an Aulopus or an Apsimar. I may be related to the great Cerularius, but the rumours that I might be of Cuman or Patzinak descent are without foundation. It cannot be doubted that my great-grandfather was under-secretary to the Catapan of Longobardia, and a remote uncle was, briefly, a Drungarius. I am, perhaps, an Argyri or Tzintziloukes at several removes, but it was always my policy to be circumspect and subtle. I did not involve myself in politics, for I valued my eyes and my tongue, and I wished to father children, yet it seems I have offended the third Panhypersebastus of the wardrobe, and so I find myself in these regions to the south of Dyrrachium, where the only amusements are the periodic incursions of the accursed Zupan of Raskia.

The olives of Bithynia cannot be obtained here, and the local varieties are very small and bitter. Sirs, imagine my misery: a year has passed since I received word from the capital, and should I be lost forever to civilised society, marooned like a new Ovid in Scythian wastes, my eyes would always look back to that far beacon with the yearning of a child for some bright toy hidden from him by an evil nurse; for I was born, I am proud to say, in that incomparable thrice-blessed, God-guarded place, and there I would wish to die if only you—most exalted Protonobilissimus, and most majestic Protopanenthimohypertatus—would once again admit me within its invincible walls. In the Name of Our Saviour, let me return to the bosom of my Mother, the City. Then you would see how I would cover her with devout kisses (ah yes, kissing the very stones and statues, the incriptions . . .), how I would praise her with inexhaustible eulogies of my own composition. Also, I could tell you of many seditions . . .

Misconception of Richness

A step out of the upper air through a space
like the lounge of a luxurious hospital—
you were standing on the wrong side of the world,
at the wrong end of the year, and you liked it at once.

It was something strange and familiar
like a new soul song that fits its year and season
perfectly and is then forgotten, but remains
like tinsel hooked on the spines of an ancient conifer.

That woman's voice, so bright and clouded. A gift of the air—
nocturnal perfumes built steep, blue terraces above
a sea of idleness. These were the flowers
of January, and I did not know their names.

Is it important to know whether
this has happened, is happening, or will happen?
For weeks, for months I have pursued the incidents of a dream
thinking they were real—they were so ordinary—

only to give up the search for lack
of corroboration: A could not have been there,
B would never have said such a thing,
and C was still a child, incapable of speech,

and yet she had explained my grief to me
in phrases of magnificent clarity. There was no cure.
In a park poised like a balcony above the ocean
the displays of nineteenth-century horticulturists

had vanished, but photographs dimly preserved them.
The light was clear, then luminously grey. Seals

lolled on the rocks below, lords of their domain,
and I stayed for a week in a suburb built

on sand dunes. I liked the architecture—
the pastel gables and Hispanic extravagances,
but felt that they might shift at any moment,
and the hill subside into the garden

with no more fuss than a dreamer or drunkard
rolling out of bed onto a worn carpet. From
my window I could see the red flowers of the quince
blazing against the uneven grey slats of the fence.

Indomitable beauties, enjoying sunlight when they can,
they still get by with little, but if brought indoors
and forced, their flowers fade almost to white, the white
of celadon. Keeping their original vividness

only as memory or echo, they are what I know
from dim gardens in Europe, yet here they seem
more darkly attended, linked to the ships' horns sounding
through fog that forestalled the sunset, and the city

covers with a cloak of muffled light more hills
than are in Jerusalem or Rome. There once was
a great hope, somewhere nearby, thousands rushed to—
it echoes still in winter sunlight, flowers and fog.

Three Scenes

1.

Indigence like a fog infects
the folkloric woodlands and trailers.
An axe is heard. Insects
descend at evening toward
the magnet of her very pale arm
from which the woollen shawl
has slipped. The atmosphere is
good/not good for the child.
Sometimes a violin or bird
screeches its two wrong notes nightlong.

The empty cashbox sinks in the clear river.
How far away is the city? No matter
how far, it is time to be going.

The city is distant by many waterways and islands.
Its towers rise beside a bay.
Each ferry has a different
name and colour. Let us travel
on the blue *Berenice,*
the white *Irene,* the lonely *Anna.*
The child will laugh at the waves/
the child will scream and hide itself
in the Greek folds of the shawl.
There will be a sound like an axe falling.

2.

The woman's hair is like a lion's mane.
In the café, in a whisper, she tells the child
the story of the travelling salesman's ghost.

Rain falls slant against the elevated train.
At noon the light remains dim. The tear in
the window blind is big enough for one blue eye.

Between flower beds in the shape of sunbursts
the local militia stand at attention. The statues
seem to say, "There's always a war somewhere."

The summer is vanishing back into cement.
A sanitation truck passes, plastered with leaves.
In the square the yellow tents are folded.

The murderer complains that his mother never loved him,
and continues: "You have to go to the edge,
and when you get there you can't go no further." Yes,

and the trick is to walk elegantly, without shuddering
above the girders, and garbage and distant fires.
Word is, "down there they drown you in your car."

3 .
Caught up in the concerns of the day
(a mild Wednesday in October) he resolved
to stay where he was and think about these matters.
It had been a year of disturbances, storms out of season.

Or he decided to set out at once for the mountains
and the snows, a place beneath a blue pine . . .
Surely a life of the instincts was preferable to
the rehearsal of Hellenistic philosophies?

Sitting on the warm stones of the harbour,
he reflected: "All decisions are hazardous,

including the decision not to decide. To know
the names of all the boats and to have consulted

the long-range forecasts is not enough, nor
to be enchanted by maps showing the ragged
outlines of glaciers and fjords, nor to think
of star-like flowers under the hooves of elk,

when your heart cannot ignore the new towers
of the city, clad in red marble and black glass.
Is it possible to abandon these atriums,
these concert halls, cafés and record stores?

Regarded coldly, the choices look meagre:
a) moving on, b) staying put, c) personal extinction,
and d) turning back, which is equivalent to c) . . ."
On the esplanade contented couples strolled

toward a lurid conflagration in the west,
unperplexed by dull-witted abstractions
that grazed above their heads. A woman
        turned to him and asked: "What keeps us here,

where the very air seems a menace? There is
no war, yet the streets are littered with the dying,
and to take a walk is to step on outstretched hands."
He replied: "There are reasons for disquiet.

There are rumours of a plot against the Boss,
and a new outbreak of Platonism has alarmed

the clerics, yet your desire for a haven seems
a possible regression, a romance of sturdy hill forts

after plague has emptied the cities; but this is not
such an age, not yet. We are alive here and living.
Let us go home while it is still light. Let us
behave in the manner of travellers returning."

After five years' absence how much smaller the town seems, and
    richer—
How much the ideal country-cottage aesthetic has come to
    dominate!
One half expects to see a flock of sheep in every garden.
Permanent exile is definitely an option.

*

I lived in suburbs so long
I may never get over it, but now I am in love
With the memory of certain peculiar chrysanthemums.
I stand on the stones of a path and I drown.

*

Do I have to drag you away from your bar or book?
There are so many unimportant things to be attended to,
And a few very important ones. We will start with tonight's meal.

*

The many pairs of lovers in the botanical gardens
Do not seem to mind the passersby. If you are alone,
They will even allow you to smoke a cigarette by the fountain.

*

   To the confusion of the casual visitor, the city of S— contains an
old cathedral like a fortress, a new cathedral like a theatre, and a
prison like a cathedral. This will give you some idea of the elevated
wisdom of its inhabitants.

*

The bungalows drift off indifferently
And sink in the reservoir. Only
The carefully tended rose beds remain
on the surface, sailing purposefully onward.

*

Was that a *real* silk tie he was wearing? Be that as it may,
He remarked to his bored companion: "It is time to leave.

The chestnuts are in heavy flower." And a car backfired in the
street.

*

In the ruins by the side of the ravine, a gleaming new bathroom.

*

He says he will catch the two o'clock train from New York to
Philadelphia—
The fool! Philadelphia is a town in western Asia Minor.
Manuel Palaeologus sat on a white horse before its walls and
wept.

*

I am pleased to discover that there is a town in Turkey called
Batman.
Alas, it is surrounded by oil wells and is entirely unpicturesque.

*

Portuguese night, Aegean night, Manhattan night, Pacific
night—
O night like a tattered curtain reluctant to descend!
Moon! Lovely as a Korean grocery store at midnight . . .

*

There were once poets everywhere hereabouts. Impossible to
compute the number of street signs and baroque plaques commem-
orating them. A whole family of them lived for generations in the
drowned convent of Santa Clara, but, alas, they have all moved
away, perhaps as a result of the frequent disputes over matters of
style that so often degenerated into devastating street brawls.
Things got so bad that the cafés became uninhabitable, but the
discriminating tourist may still admire the ruins of the Tower of the
Poets, the Fountain of the Poets, the Palace of the Poets, the Race-
course of the Poets and the Abbatoir of the Poets. Indeed, on
occasion, a slim volume can still be found poking out of a mound
of rubble. But, of course, if you find one you must at once report it
to the ministry.

*

On the insignificant hill above my hometown
Giant concrete letters spell out the name
BEETHOVEN.
The campaign to replace it with the name
KOECHLIN or the name MERIKANTO
Seems doomed to failure. Ah, such noble names!
And I had hoped to put the place on the map.

                        *

Dear sir, I am most gratified to learn
From your letter that you have fallen in love
More passionately than ever before in your experience,
But I must assure you that this has absolutely nothing
To do with anything I might have said, even in public.

                        *

   The child who still hadn't learnt that the statues could not re-
spond stood by the green pool (in which a family of goldfish were
quarrelling over a crust of bread) shouting Athena! Adonis! Ac-
taeon! while his mother called his name impatiently from the gate.

                        *

I grieve for the place I left behind.
I smile on the place where I am.
But the place where I am going—
Well, that is a different matter.

                        *

   His lovely red-haired wife having died giving birth to them, a
man discovered that his twin children—a girl and a boy—were ge-
niuses. Without any teaching they composed music and poetry, and
early on showed an interest in philosophy and the natural sciences.
Their paintings took the form of mysterious allegories concerning
which connoisseurs spilt futile rivers of ink.
   Their father loved them absolutely, yet feared that they might
not respect him, but they were so truly intelligent that they under-

stood that their father—though less gifted than they and some-
times a little foolish—was nevertheless a good man. He, for his
part, perceived in all their works the many colours of their mother's
hair and skin, the gleam her green eyes had on certain evenings.

*

Intoxicated by history and the weather
I walked all around the city today,
And because it is so hilly I am exhausted,
Even though the whole place is no bigger than a garden.

*

The dust on my shoes surely deserves investigation.
In general it must be said that the dust here
Is of an exceptionally high quality.

*

In this country of orange groves, orange roofs and rice paddies
It took me some time to understand the ways of the maids.
In the first week they will mislay your laundry willfully,
Replacing it with that of some wealthy financier or property
     developer,
And of course you cannot go out in these preposterous
     garments—
It would be better to go naked. In the second week
They will perhaps deliver the beautifully laundered robes and
     headgear
Of a Tibetan lama, and this is an improvement—
One can at least go out to a café dressed in this fashion.
In the third week a subtle understanding is reached,
And a handsome necktie appears amid the sleek folds of evening
     gowns.

*

O night as full of perfume as a mountain of flowering bushes,
You are the victim of several cunning grafts,
Which, I fear, can hardly be considered lawful.

*

The grandmother in her black dress
Gathers her beautiful granddaughter to her breast
(Where a sickle moon hangs from a long chain)
And says: "My darling, you must not sleep
With attractive young men, for they will write you sonnets,
They will write you whole sequences of despairing lyrics in *vers
libre*.
So you see it would be terribly cruel of you to share their beds."
And the granddaughter glances toward
The volume of despairing sonnets
Burning in her raincoat pocket.

*

O expeditions in red and white sports cars, you resemble a
rondo!

*

By old flowering walls that long afternoon
Winter and the anxieties of great cities seemed
Nothing more than superstitions our reason had dismissed.

*

As if we stood on some Acropolis
The view was uninterrupted for many miles.
It opened like a fan with stars in its spokes.

*

I was sitting on my balcony one evening trying to trace the
source of a particularly strong odour of honeysuckle when suddenly
a bugle began to blow, and an enormous image of Hercules ap-
peared in the sky. What a hero! He leaned so close I could feel his
breath, which was hot and smelled of oregano, but I did not like

the gleam in his eye, and ran quickly into the house, slamming the shutters behind me.

I picked up a book I had been reading. Everything was calm again. Freya Stark was still sailing along the coast of Lycia. I ignored the loud thumping on the shutters.

Methodical Sonatas

As if encarmined tulips opened
with a sudden pop like that of a toy pistol
morning surprises you again,
and the new griefs already seem the old griefs
and they must move over, shift seats
in this mismanaged theatre of a life
so that the fresh pain may be installed
like a blade of glass next to the wrists.

The page no longer lies flat, it blinks and rises.
The words assume green or yellow vestments,
and officiously obstruct the way forward
like secretaries in some bland outer office,
refusing to remember your name:
you are invisible again
as if standing at a bar in England.

A sudden shock or surge, an overload,
something as simple as a snowfall
on the grid of civilised barbarity
and you can't even retrieve the name
of the houseplant nodding on the sill—

it is somewhere in the lost tenth chapter
of the two-volume novel about the catastrophe of modernity—
our divorce from everything prior to the invention
of the gramophone.

Evening is coming on like a wave
and the hatches have not been secured.
The past leaks in and the ship goes down.
The rescue attempts are conducted under
rapidly advancing banks of purple cloud.

It's true you can get used to anything,
even dawn at evening, but surely
something should be done to revise the programme
and patch up the hole in the sky? Sadly
the lamentations sound routine and promises
to do better in the future had best be discounted,
since this *is* the future and we are living it,
second by second, breathlessly, in the hope
of some connection between notes.

"I am sorry I could not come to your assistance,
but I was in danger of drowning as well,
and the shattered glass rained about my head,
so I write this letter to you—you who are dead—
and drop it into the loud surf amid which
I clearly see your attentive ear lying like a shell."

Weekends in
West Connecticut

It is a place of enormous trees
and a million stridulant insects.
At the center of so much counterpoint
sleep is impossible, and the garden is crushed
into something like a pill the night will swallow.

Of course the light still loiters in the streets,
and the houses with their varied porches are charming
as musical boxes filled with *Rückert* lieder,
but what is it causes this putative mayor of Westport
and his wife to decorate their master bedroom
with crude agricultural implements?
It looks like a torture chamber . . . Outside,

blue spruces, red oaks, white pines all loom,
and the undergrowth's lush and tangled as Mandarin prose.
You imagine boundless forests, but the path is barred
a short way in at the outer precincts of another shrine
to domesticity, glowing through mutinous leaves,
and the sun, forgotten token, drops somewhere out of sight.

Nothing is held in common here:
corporations build their headquarters beside
absurd, idyllic millponds, and the city towers,
the open lands are driven away,
ever further over the unglimpseable horizon.
Confused by so much opulence and uniformity
it would be easy to forget the way out,
easy to forget that such a thing was needed.

A land without horizon or sunset is a safe place—
safe as the bedroom of your childhood
with its yellow walls and deceiving pictures

of friendly grownups and loquacious animals,
but when the last bricks of these walls have crumbled,
when the last shreds of those images have been blown
into the ocean, you are left alone in the muggy garden
with the irritable cat, amid a swarm of cries.

You hold in your hand a guide to
Swedish folk art in America.

Merikanto's Concerto

Somewhere in Finland a composer sits
like a clock or a primrose
surrounded by a thousand lakes and snow.
Perhaps this is always the situation, or
it is quite possible that he is enveloped
by summer light, endless sunsets
and irritating swarms of gnats.

His summer house would be made of wood?
His apartment looks out from classical windows?
Alighting on the staves, the gnats
have their own ideas about music,
and at once the largo breaks into a scherzo.

It is the 1920s. A little further to the east
Elizabeth Södergram's beloved and beautiful
long-haired cat is shot dead by her neighbour
for the crime of urinating on his roses.
Many sad poems result from the event,
and the composer, meanwhile, is cutting whole pages
out of his orchestral masterpiece. Perhaps
he cuts them into shreds like straw, and a bird
carries them off to make its nest. The students
find nothing. Who can say—O tangible air
of a far landscape, eternally refreshed?
Who can account for it?

A blizzard has passed over the score
obliterating landmarks. True,
the climate is sympathetic only
to Sibelius and Brahms, to
the benighted imitators of Sibelius and Brahms, *but,*
as we say in a kind of uncomprehending grief

for what is lost and we will never hear, *even so* . . .
couldn't he have waited before resorting
to folk song and neoclassicism,
before writing in the margins
"unplayable, may it remain so"?

Oblivion is eager, Ondine,
but for now we have the victory.
It is the 1990s in America
on a burning day in summer, in the stinking
oven of the city, and for a few moments
the opening melody of Merikanto's concerto
holds all our attention like a very white
and radiant curtain being slowly drawn aside—

A History of Soviet Organ Music

The boy is in the field,
and the new tractor is there, gleaming.
Tears spring to his eyes. An organ sounds,
and this causes some uncertainty
in the audience, since the very existence
of Soviet organ music had been something
entirely unsuspected until this moment.
And the boy is a marionette,
and the tractor only a careful construction
of blue cornflowers and straw, even though
the corn continues golden for miles over the black earth,
as far as Kazan or vanished Itil of the Khazars!

The history of Soviet organ music
is easily told: from the time of its foundation
in the tenth century, the Russian church
has found no use for the organ whatsoever.
Thus the Soviet organ is a youthful organ
heard to best advantage in lively medleys
of traditional Uzbek melodies—
and, oh, how blue the cornflowers, how black
the earth, how red the kerchief of the female comrade!
The younger brother of the heroic youth, meanwhile,
is having a fit of hysterics on the Ferris wheel
which turns and turns to the accompaniment
of Soviet organ music.

Some Words of Advice:
After Hesiod

Never believe the words you hear in popular songs.
Conversely, believe them all,
even the ones about changing the world and living forever.

If you habitually rise early and take a run around the park,
make sure that, on certain days, you sleep past noon.
(This advice is reversible.) Staying in bed all day
watching the snow fall with a pain in your belly
is not recommended, but a lot of soup is good,
and vigorous dreaming of architecture. If, nevertheless,

you have to worry, confine your worrying
to one subject: money is always a good choice.
Never worry about "the absurdity of existence,"
or similar large vaguenesses which are really like
the memory of a grandmother who died before you were born.
What good will it do you? And do not become enslaved to
      anything.

There are other more specific forms of advice. For example,
if you go to a party and the apartment in which it is being held
resembles a hotel lobby, or a fashionable gallery,
leave immediately. Also avoid at all cost
people who ask questions like: "What kind of poetry
do you write?" or "What's it like to live in Manchester?"

If you believe that God is good and drink innately evil,
do not try to convince your friends. You will find
that even in the most crowded social gatherings
a wide circle opens around you. You will be left
puzzling at the large abstract painting on the wall.

Music may surround you like an enormous blue and rose-streaked
    sky,
But, if you prefer Wagner to Mozart, you are probably in
    trouble.
A soul singer's voice may convince you that the future is a
    promise
that will be kept, but the average day is doubts
with a kind of half-assed, upbeat effect at the end.

But don't be disgusted.
It's time to get readjusted.

My Book of Evasive Moves
is published by *Apocrypha Press Ltd.,*
a wholly-owned subsidiary of
Inaction Universal
and you should read it today,
but I must ask you to wait for my epic novel
Discarded Lovers, which will contain
everything you need to know: it is at least
three volumes long, and unwritten.

Several Romantic Novels

Before the body that almost destroyed them, masters of
 eloquence gape merely.
There are no words for this, or too many words that never quite
 fit—
each a Cinderella's shoe to these blunt objects of sense. *Exempla:*
The door opened with a sigh. You had forgotten you had left it
 unlocked—
and at the dark end, like a funnel, of such a cold day! This is
 something to be watched,
yet negligence can allow sudden reversals into summer heat even
 as winter advances:
a cardinal attempts, with its one steel note, to stitch the garden
 back together,
fastening a geranium to a shirt of snow. But the bird stays
 hidden.
Does it matter who entered? His arrival is, anyway, a gust,
 pushing you back
into a chamber of distorted perspective, of distorting mirrors,
 and the one
who has arrived follows, becomes concentrated like a pillar while
 your body disperses—
a hand like a torn flag, an eye big as a geographer's globe, your
 neck
a leaning tower about to fall into as many pieces as there are
 leaves on the unswept lawn.
How long can this shuddering continue? The autumn slows. The
 hours cannot withstand it.
It travels under the skin of highways whose trees seem studded
 with garnets, with blood-droplets;
even the truck stops are quaking, and the prairie of the dog
 convulses into ravines
vaulted by fire, floored with glass, until you arrive at the summit
 of a rock formation

resembling a steamboat, but some miles from any river.
                                        Below (below deck)
a thousand fabulous dinner parties are in progress and, unaware
of what is happening to the landscape, your host proffers, in
        greeting, his wooden hand.
He is a stranger to you, as are all his guests so happily absorbed
        in
the convivial mood-music and margaritas when, to you, it seems
        time
to talk of *the irrational,* time to make an opera out of the
        earthquake,
even as the prongs penetrate the breasts of the enormous dead
        bird,
and some damned Vivaldi concerto stutters into life like a
        knitting machine.
The urge to shout "Fire!" or at least, "Look, *I'm* on fire!"
        becomes irresistible,
yet, in truth, these are the kindest and most charming of
        people—so
much so that I think all their children must be chamber-
        musicians—
and this is the kindest and most charming of towns, a town of
        porch swings and pumpkin-lanterns
wherein the most deviant perspectives, the most grotesque
        peccadilloes are
tethered securely to the gold cupola of the capitol. There is
        nothing to fear,
the citizens are on watch and will surely return the scattered
        parts of your body
should they find them: "I recognize this, sir, as your penis. You
        left it
on a bench in the mall, close by a cut-price shoe outlet, I
        believe." So

perhaps it is O.K. to leave your door ajar again if that is your
     mood,
only remember there are some violent natural phenomena that
take the form of men or women. (*He* was a cyclone at least; he
     has returned
to a remote state with a name like that of sexual lubricant.)
     Other
instances might be offered of which the scream of a damaged car
     heater
would be one, but for now what you had thought forgotten
     covers the occasion like a mantle—
evening assuming a profounder blue, the dead awaking in a
     glance,
and it is time to be attentive, watching for the apparition of a
     red bird,
for the green bowl of the garden to fill with snow. There
     remains
the no one who came and the no one who departed, his growing
     legend.

Popular Mechanics:
2 Poems on the Same Theme

1. Realistic
The clouds were moving fast
the day I moved in here. I recall
the flying trash and crippled umbrellas
in the public bins. First off
I put the TV out on the sidewalk.
It vanished within minutes. It was too big
and the wrong colour: I felt *it* was watching *me* . . .
But now, with snow beginning to fall,
I wonder, was I wise? Should I update myself
with the wisdom of talk-show hosts
and their oracular guests—
buy a VCR so I can watch *Huge 2*
or *Like a Horse, Popular Mechanics*
or *Dynastud?* Don't say no.
These guys, who are extremely handsome,
are giving their all, giving and taking it for so long
it's hard to credit. There's something here
beyond the call of duty, like bringing flowers
as well as doing the dishes. *Turned on*
also seems an apt term. We are returned to
the early years of the Industrial Revolution—
pistons and cogs, balls and weights and steam,
a mechanical image of the constellations.

In this dream-come-true the new stable boy
gladly answers the young master's lust,
and anyone attractive on the airplane,
in the lumberyard, or at the black-tie dinner
complies without a second thought: *simple
and faithless as a shake of the hand.*

2 . Ideal

Fast forward or freeze, the film
is still an idyll in which we are once again
impulsive and free. It seems strange
that such graphic actions should serve illusion,
yet they do, and it may be at a price. It is
always at a price. The gods are always raging,
blue in the face, jealous of mortal beauty.
They see how it can alter, how it can include
imperfection. Often a person is beautiful,
not because they resemble Hyacinth,
but because we remember the room or garden
where we just saw them; we see the light
that first surrounded them, the leaves
amid which they laughed—

that summer, that sky, this night
when the flesh fits the skull perfectly,
as it always has, like a necklace fits
a particular throat that reminds us
of a tall column in the Doric style.

In the glow of these features
we cannot think of dying: it is
something that must never happen—
a baroque embarrassment. Yet
the bruises also glow. The sky
above the city tonight is a great bruise
of dull violet and dull grey and dull yellow.
We desire the actors we cannot touch,
and they undress before us like roses.
But when the human undresses

it is the assumption of leaves and roses,
cared for and unseen, only existing
as the arm of a statue does in a forgotten place
where the leaves are blowing and the sunlight falls,
as it must, violently, upon the walls and the windows.

The Middle Kingdom

In those days we spent our time
sitting quietly in softly lighted rooms
designed for that purpose, trying not
to let any involuntary line of thought
arrive at its logical (and, of course,
regrettable) conclusion: namely,
that our days were numbered.

We were all well-fed and warmly clothed,
and experienced no misgivings on this account.
The oceans were calm and shallow,
the rivers stocked with salmon. Each spring
brilliantly coloured birds passed over
on their way to northern lakes and hills.
Poems were often penned concerning
their brief and glorious transit. When
they returned in autumn we succumbed
to appropriate feelings of mild regret.

Our figurative art gave no hint of the fact
that male animals experienced erections,
nor were children obliged to light the match
that would incinerate their families.
Similarly it was not considered necessary
to rip your opponent's lips from his face,
or force him to digest his ears.

How slow that time now seems,
how sweet, how gradual every graceful gesture!
But it is impossible to regret its passing
It was not a time of truth and realism.
The passage of migratory birds
did not accord to the facts, nor

the coming of spring, nor the love of mothers
for their children, nor a man's respect
for women, nor courtesy, friendship, honour . . .

Regret is impossible
(and, besides, nostalgia
is an imprisonable offense) now
that every issue is clear as blood,
bright as tears, and we live
in understanding even as we die.

HRGB *or A Lunar Eclipse in Yemen*

In his description of the trade route to India
Pliny mentions in passing "Sapphar,
residence of the king," and this is the first
certain reference in the western sources to
the fabled, nine-gated city of the Himyarites.
At about the same time, the unknown author
of the *Periplus of the Erythraean Sea*
(doubtless a merchant captain long familiar
with the routes that led from Alexandria
to India by way of south Arabia)
describes Zafar as "the residence of Charibael,
king of the Homerites and Sabaites,"
and it may have been this same Charibael,
or one of his immediate successors
who first assumed the sonorous title
"King of Saba and Lord of Raydan" (there is
no mention of Himyar or the Himyarites),
but so irresistibly splendid was the title
that it was soon adopted by all the kings
of the region, and each, as was natural,
hotly contested the claims of his rivals.

Above the hill a shadow begins to cross the moon.
Gunfire sounds from the mountains. Fires are lit.
The people make a great noise with pots and pans and firecrackers.

Perhaps the king of Himyar conquered Saba,
or the king of Saba conquered Himyar,
but it is safe to assume that the true "King
of Saba and Lord of Raydan" must always
have resided in the palace of Raydan,
in the city of Zafar, in the land of Himyar.
Here, the poet-king abu-Karib Asad received

ambassadors from Axum or Byzantium,
under an arch from whose spandrels Winged Victories
in turbulent robes extended tiaras. If
this was not Raydan, it was Kawkabatan
(so called because it was adorned with white stones
resembling stars), or Dhu Yazan, or Shawbatan—
the work of King Malikkarib and his sons,
who caused its walls to be panelled with mosaics,
and exotic woods so magnificent that
it was said to be the work of djins. For Zafar
is remembered as a city of many palaces,
and the most splendid of them was the one we know,
from an inscription of difficult terminology,
only by the letters HRGB.
It was built for King Sharahbil Yafur
in the year 457, and his inscription boasts
of pillared arcades, alabaster windows,
gilded bells and statues of lions,
all of which the king piously dedicated
to "the Merciful Lord of Heaven and Earth."
Whether the Lord so addressed was the God
of the Jews or the Christians we do not know,
but it is all too apparent that He showed
small mercy to Himyar in the years that followed.

A shadow is crossing the moon—
reddish-brown and burnt like sugar.
The echo of gunfire sounds in the valleys.
The flames leap up, the firecrackers sputter.

At Marib the great dam failed. In neither
Himyar nor Saba was there skill to repair it.

In the Temple of Almaqah the kings had long ceased
to erect memorials. The Ethiopians
were in Zafar. The last king of Himyar of whom
we have certain knowledge is one Dhu Nuwas,
or "Lord of Curls." Fired by religious zeal,
he gathered an army and advanced upon Zafar.
There the church was destroyed. In Najran
forty thousand Christians were slaughtered.
The Lord of Curls exulted in his success,
and praised his God, but word of these crimes
reached the ear of Justin in the City of Constantine.
The Autocrat of All the Romans had ways to deal
with these matters. Embassies were sent to Axum,
and in the year 525 the Lord of Curls
was killed in battle, and with him died Zafar
Himyar and Saba. And Justin, in his turn,
exulted in the triumph of the True Faith.

O Almaqah, you are wholly dark now
as if covered by a robe. A long silence follows
in which the smoke of firecrackers,
the smoke of bonfires inconsequently drifts.
The people go into their houses. They attend to the cooking.

In the style of a scholar or a conqueror
one might lament the vacancy of Raydan's courts,
but to walk amid the rubble on the hill of Zafar,
in the place of Shawbatan and Kawkabatan, to step
between the letters H, R, G, and B is to read,
in the broken sentences of stones exquisitely carved,
quite another story, one that was a mystery
even to those who first framed, with stylised vines,

a scene of nude heroes riding winged leopards.
We may not know why so many "scenes abound with griffins,"
or why a bull's horns should sprout into graceful branches,
but these images speak of delight, of a land that was,
indeed, "fortunate" as the Romans had it.

My Egypt

The street is a horn the wind blows through—
a ram's horn, a car's horn, a French horn,
but its melody, though plangent, may not be
the one you want to hear right now.

The river tows its dreams,
consigned to the dim edge of existence,
reciting dull epics to desolate piers.
Many, you included, are still abed,
but already the avenues are crowded
with people like flags of more nations
than exist in the world. It is all
a pageant of some kind, though anxious
and colder than of late.

The last tropical rainstorms visit us.
It is a day in September full of whispers of anticipation.
It is a time of greetings like farewells and farewells like greetings.
For a depressing moment things seem foreordained,
entered in the prophetic ledger like age and decrepitude—
the thought of white hair and rising snowbanks,
burdened trees breaking with a crack.

Book of summer we have read you,
every word, and memorized the lines we need.
The colours turn. A single tree is purple, green and red,
and we begin to wonder if something really spectacular
will happen, like the installation on an endless
Von Sternberg staircase of the emperor or empress
of these events. We also wonder *how* it can happen
in times when the remarkable is expected, as the sun is expected
to rise, and even this seems to happen in memory—

memory which is endlessly revised
to suit the present image, to which the past
leads us by means of a strict gothic perspective.
How to account therefrom for your continual dreams
of the future which thrill and frighten you
like bombs dropping on the city of your birth?
A department store where, perhaps, your first pyjamas
were purchased goes up in flames, and the surviving streets
are black with a kind of joyful malice that is soon erased.

What are these flurries? Of snow? These heaps
of stuff, soiled or destined to melt? Mush of potsherds?
Glass of a mosaic? They are discarded in time like shoes or old
    books.
The seasons are like a day stretched over a year,
impossible to grasp, but we will be changed
at the turning of the year, changed for the better.

Scenes from Schumann

As in an old memoir, the rhododendrons were over.
Hunger persisted, and the light was weak—
the light of music and books, the light paintings cast
on bowls of fruit and tablecloths, to make them ours . . .

So the black dish was upturned,
and a fragment of it rolled with the peaches into
burnt grass nearby. It had been a long summer, and now
a glass vase in the shape of a hand stood up against

the perspective of hills and rain, dogs and daylilies.
We had known about the storm, perhaps for a century
before it happened, so much had been gathered in, protected
under awnings and arcades, yet the paintings were streaked,

and the scores curled into oblivion. It was impossible
to imagine the birth of the orchestra, as we once knew it:
it was a friend who had become many strangers, each
with a hat or facial feature, a scream or sigh

like the opening of a door that must remain shut.
We were all looking out from the windows of the library
toward the river that is not a river. The narrow lawn
looked very green after the rains, and the white chairs

were night-animals caught in searchlights.
The urns showed well against the blue of the river,
and beyond them, the ruins of the old insane asylum,
covered in leaves, in the bronze colour of their bricks—

fading, as the lights came on in loops along the bridge,
festive as the illuminations of childhood. But

the vignettes were out of focus, the anecdotes faltered; the words
took off like birds from our lips, to circle an absence

that couldn't be named without turning the feast to ashes.
Not that the talk died. No, it grew brighter, like lights reflected
in swift, dark water. Only, at intervals, we seemed to hear
the river recalling the desolate passage of a bridal barge.

Smoke

It was late in the year
and forests were burning a long way off,
the day the smoke arrived, almost unperceived.
It came as a ghost, as many ghosts,
visible in the mouths of tunnels.

Now that your neighbour is dead,
you recall casual greetings on the stairs,
snatches of show tunes in corridors,
and you look down into that well—

that well of uncertain light and air—and see an absence
which neither snow nor corrosive rain efface,
and the absence returns your glance, it follows like a cur
extending its tongue of smoke toward your hand.

The smoke enters the lamplight and the bed.
The eyes are clouded, the eyes are abolished,
and the ears that drank in the old arias of desire.
Venice is diminished, and Rome,

their bells dulled, their restaurants emptied;
in Manhattan the towers shrink from the sky;
all places and all scenes become the less observed,
the less heard, the less loved.

In a city of burnt throats there can never be
enough sweet water to start the songs
and if you would dance, you must dance to the memory
of that lighted window the dusk carried off,

those hands preparing the evening meal,
skeletal hands fumbling among

the bottles of useless prophylactics,
those limbs and mouths, smoke we daily breathe.

But don't vanish, don't take the path to the river.
It is cold there and lonely,
and the sky is a burnt page. Stay—

you and you others. If we are not to become
a dispersed people of smoke,
the monument that is us must be built soon.

The Sweeping Gesture

in the sky was final above
the hospital that was the colour of bread.
The pigeons cooed and made a home
under the fire escape. Emptiness

like a permanent echo
remained in the streets, although the ghosts
of punks and panhandlers hovered
in the improvised bazaars,
stepping between photographs of limbs
splayed and bronzed, or torsos
uniformly "god-like" in repose.

Another classic scene. The question arose:
"If the people in the city dress as if
for the beach, what do they wear at the beach?
What pleasure is there in continual
freedom from restraints?" The grid
is dropped over all colours and complaints,
and assigns to each its portion and locale.
The wind lifts the trash a little way to where
the sun sears the rose leaves, and a hand
reaches for the warm drink that was cool
a moment ago. —O air,
for some weeks absent from these shores! . . .

It is too early to leave and far beyond the point
when departure would have made a difference. You
sigh at this but continue packing anyway:

"On the island there are trees, and above them
are houses open to the slightest movement of the air,
and red-winged birds come to rest

on the weathered railings of their decks; under
the trees tunnels run from the ocean to the bay,
and all day we see what comes and goes away.
Only, over Babylon, a dull cloud hangs."

So much for letters home
(the kind that are never sent).
There must be more to it than heaven or hell,
our dirt and their purity, something
that could stand contradiction
without collapsing in a frenzy,
but you are already more cool and distant
than a waterfall: you were never here,
never belonged in these streets and avenues
when a single tree's survival seems
a miracle—and they are here
in thousands, the planes, the honey locusts,
veiling the high cornices of rusticated
tenements, the smiling capitals of wealthy houses.

All the other places that come to mind
(possible locations of other lives
that might have been ours with a change of luck)
are neither exotic nor blessed:
they too are a part of what we call *home*—
towers and bridges, wild flowers, boulevards,
mountains and demolished smokestacks,
and however far away the singer may be
the song still arrives with news from the hotel
of the red quilt a mother stitched with stars.

It is time for these things to be part of understanding,
for mere opinion and impotent rage to diminish

to a murmur, a background harmony like the sob
of an off-stage horn, time for the art of illumination
to be revived in golden air. Already the small, blue
ferryboat puts out from the dock toward home or the city.

Minutes of silence are observed with every dawn
and the buildings grow taller with the news of each loss.

Following a Man

I was following a man
with a handsome, intelligent face
(the cheekbones high, the nose straight, the lips
sufficiently full), and judging by the shape
of his neck (an unfailingly reliable
indicator in my experience) a lithe, athletic
figure; or, to be more exact, he and I were merely walking
in the same direction along Seventh Avenue,
having earlier stood side by side in the Old Chelsea Post Office:
the day was Friday, June 9th, the time late afternoon,
and after only two or three blocks,
each full of its particular events and distractions
(such as dogs, clouds, paupers, hydrants, hairdressers),
I began to feel that I was almost in love with this man,
that, like a song, I would follow him anywhere . . .

Something about the way he slicked back his hair
delighted me, and I admired his beautiful raincoat
which so enhanced the easy masculine grace
of his movements. I was concentrating hard,
trying to take in all these details without giving
any cause for embarrassment (either on my part
or his) when he swerved into a newspaper store
between 16th Street and 15th, and I could think of no
plausible excuse for following him into that meagre space
where, surely, our eyes would have been forced to meet,
and I would have blushed (he being protected by a light tan).

In all likelihood he is lost to me, as
he would have been had that door been
the door to an elevator in an apartment building
bigger than all the pyramids combined.
Even if he should prove to be my near-neighbour

I doubt that I will ever see him again,
since in New York there are always too many
neighbours to keep track of (you hear
their footsteps, their voices and their music,
but it is difficult to attach these attributes
to a particular person, in much the same way
that an archaeologist may uncover the fragments
of a mirror but will never know the face
that, day by day, was reflected there)
but it is not as if he were dead. He exists
and will continue to do so for some time, perhaps
for many years, and as I walked without hesitation
directly past the store he had entered I was overcome
with a sudden feeling of elation at the thought
that it was within my power to record this incident
which is unexceptional
as the budding of pear trees in their season,
unrepeatable as the first sight of a great city.

Cigarettes

Problems of translation are, perhaps, not so great
between languages as between different versions
of the same language. Why, for example, does
"fag" mean homosexual in America, when,
in England, it means cigarette? Does this imply
that those who first observed the phenomenon
of smoking in the New World were homosexual?
This would cause some consternation on Columbus Day,
and, in all likelihood, the assumption is unjustified,
since Columbus and his crew were not English-speakers.
Yet, if we dismiss the idea of happy crowds of
homosexual Spanish or Italian mariners
returning to Europe with cigarettes in hand,
eager to introduce this new pleasure to their lovers,
we should perhaps concede that there is some connection
between the two ideas. It was Oscar Wilde, after all,
who described smoking as "the perfect pleasure, because"—
he opined—"it always leaves one unsatisfied."
It is clear from this that he was thinking of sexual pleasure,
of the working-class youths with whom he so recklessly dined
in fashionable restaurants of the eighteen-nineties.
A cigarette is like a passion in that it is inhaled deeply
and seems to fill all the empty spaces of the body,
until, of course, it burns down, and is put out amid
the shells of pistachio nuts, or whatever trash
may be at hand, and the passion may leave traces
that in time will grow malignant: he who has taken pleasure
may die many years after in the room of an anonymous
hotel or hospital, under the blank gaze of a washstand,
a bad painting or an empty vase, having forgotten entirely
the moment that announced the commencement
of his dying. And perhaps he will not understand:
it is another false translation, like someone stumbling over
the word for cigarette in a new and intolerable language.

A Dead Man Speaks of the Sky

We hear *falado,* and we are glad to know that a dead man
is speaking of the sky . . .
      —Alberto Savinio, *Speaking to Clio*

The way out is narrow and the steps broken
(But my feet have no need of them)
I imagine an ilex up there against the empty sky

Falado It is remembered
It is a page torn from a book

The roses are tangled along the path to the tomb
The painters are all dead (but their colours remain bright)
The harpist's hand is stopped forever in mid-stroke

Falado It is remembered
It is still water without a sail

Perhaps stars show through oak leaves (but I no longer
Recall the stories they once told to educated eyes)
Or summer sun drives travellers to shade

Departing swallows veer and cry above the harvest
(But it is not gathered in and fires burn where none should
    burn)
Wings still flicker over the rockface where the sisters fell

Falado It is remembered
It is a buried flagstone

The sky is a great square where the blessed wander
Those whom no one has ever chatted with beside a fountain
(But it is cold now and thin clouds announce the winter)

The city is barren where once my wife
(Bending in the posture of a mourner)
Uttered the word *aguletora* to our firstborn son

O falado It is forgotten
It is nothing and nowhere and no one

Visigothic

It had been raining all day,
and I found myself trying to imagine
the life of the Visigothic kingdom.

We know which cities were destroyed
or abandoned in the years
of confusion, but others survived,

if somewhat reduced in size,
and the building of churches and palaces
continued. Laws were propounded,

and the kings wore crowns of particular
magnificence. Nor were they indifferent
to learning, since it was during this period

that the *Etymologies* of Isidore
were composed. Life was not without
its pleasures: we know, for example,

that King Sisebut reprimanded
Bishop Eusebius of Tarraco concerning
his excessive devotion to circus shows.

I concluded that it made no sense
for us to call them "barbarians." Theirs
was not an age of unrelieved darkness.

And the rain was still falling in the airshaft,
and sirens howled, and clouds obscured the towers.
Try as I might there was little I could see

in the pages of my books except
an elegant line of narrow arches
abandoned on a hillside somewhere,

its original purpose unknown,
and a list of names I could barely
pronounce: Leovigild, Recared . . .

The Seventeenth Sermon

In the turbulent career of the patriarch Photios
there can have been few days more glorious
than Saturday, March 29th 867.
It was on this day that he delivered his seventeenth sermon,
"On the Inauguration of the Image of the Virgin,"
in the great church of the Holy Wisdom,
in the presence of the emperors Michael III and Basil I.
It was Easter, and the long night of iconoclasm—
the rule of those "shameful emperors now universally
    deplored"—
had ended. The patriarch indicated
a group of worshippers dressed all in white, men
who had recently abjured the execrable doctrines
of the Quartodecimans, according to whom Easter
should be celebrated on the fourteenth day of the lunar month,
whether or not it was a Sunday. As Photios
continued to speak with his customary eloquence and erudition,
the devout gathering could see in the apse behind him
the new image of the enthroned Virgin and her Child,
seeming to float on a gold ground, and flanked by the archangels
Michael and Gabriel. To Photios it seemed
as if the Virgin were about to speak, to explain
to any sceptics her paradoxical status as virgin and mother,
for her lips seemed of real flesh, pressed together and still
as in the sacraments. Her gaze was compassionate
yet detached, directed toward a child and eternity;
her image was a silent script from which both the learned
and the ignorant could acquaint themselves with the truths
of Christian doctrine. But a man
of Photius's intellectual refinement could not
countenance a merely didactic philosophy of art.
He did not neglect the aesthetic properties:
by its beauty and harmony of proportion

the image gave delight and strength to the spectator,
and predisposed the mind to accept the order of the universe.
All of this Photios further claimed was an act of restoration:
the church, though still scarred and wounded,
had now regained some of her ancient beauty; sadness was cast
    off,
and she was once again clothed in her bridal garment.
In this respect the patriarch was almost certainly mistaken,
since all the evidence suggests that the original decoration
of the church consisted of abstract vines and garlands
framing many simple representations of the cross.
Photius's "forms imprinted on the tablets of the soul" did not
exist in the time of Justinian and Anthemius.

In the course of his sermon the patriarch also took care
to praise Michael and Basil, calling them
"a beloved pair of pious emperors, father and son,
shining in royal purple," but according to the histories
Michael was a notorious drunkard
given to loutish acts of vandalism, while Basil,
his adopted son, was an illiterate peasant,
born of a Slav mother and an Armenian father.
His magnificent physique had caught the emperor's eye
as he was passing by the palace stables one day,
and it seems likely that the two men became lovers.
It is certain that they shared the favours
of the same woman, one Eudocia Ingerina,
and as he delivered his sermon Photios must have thought
of the fate of his benefactor, the Caesar Bardas.
It has been said in Michael's defence that although
unfit to rule he allowed better men to govern for him,
chief among them his uncle the Caesar, enlightened
founder of the new university of the Magnaura Palace,

but in the spring of the previous year Basil
had killed Bardas in the presence of the emperor,
and immediately afterward was himself raised to the throne.
In the months that followed the seventeenth sermon
the two men grew suspicious of each other.
Michael drank while Basil made plans, disposing
of Michael on the evening of September 23rd 867.
Such were the men Photios lauded as "beloved" and "pious,"
and such was the beginning of the Macedonian golden age,
for against all expectation Basil ruled wisely,
and his family held the throne for nearly two centuries,
and art and learning flourished, and magnificent churches
were built, and the borders of the empire steadily expanded.
In the eastern apse of Saint Sophia the subject
of Photios's sermon can still be seen: the Virgin's robe
is a fathomless blue, the archangels' wings exhaust the rainbow.

Braid

In the first portrait
the very small prince is wrapped
in a costume stiff with gold and silver thread.
His dwarf, who is no taller than he
but many years older, appears to lurch
out of the frame, holding the sceptre
and the other symbols of kingship. Later
we see the prince at the riding school.
He is very proud, since he has conquered a horse,
and his entire family watch him from a distant balcony.
He carries a great white plume in his hat,
under the blue and green changes of the Spanish sky.

In the last portrait,
His Highness Prince Baltasar Carlos
appears in hunting costume, a fine cap on his head.
He looks a little puzzled, but nonetheless resolute,
as he should, since he is heir to a great empire.
The landscape of that empire recedes behind him,
and in it towns are burning, ships are sinking,
and there are buffoons whose eyes are always crossed,
and somewhere an old woman is cooking eggs,
watched by the boy who holds a jar of clear oil.

Miracles occur: a raven descends
with a loaf of bread big enough for two;
lions are digging a saint's grave,
and the young Prince Baltasar Carlos
learns how to ride, learns how to hunt, how
to be a king, and dies in his seventeenth year.
His father must have wept for a day, but then,

for the good of the Hapsburg line, married his son's
betrothed. She, we understand, was sixteen and he
forty-six. This was a small matter of diplomacy.
In the portrait her cheeks are highly rouged.
Her black dress is crossed by many bands of silver braid.

Revising the Atlas

It was just something I knew and thought I'd tell you.
Its relevance might be questionable, but that is no reason
not to draw attention to it, as one might to a carnation
crushed into the tarmac by a truck. I think I got the facts right
about "the egg crown," the invasions, and the arrow that killed
the rebellious second cousin of the incestuous emperor
(who fired it, in what poison its barb was steeped),
but what are you to make of this information? I could say:
*That year the suburban palaces had to be rebuilt, for the sixth time
in a decade,* and that might produce the required sense of awe
and strangeness, also of revulsion at acts of inhumanity and
    wanton
destructiveness which, however, show no sign of stopping—
mosaic faces torn from the walls and the domes,
the little towns with no names burning all over the rumpled
    map.

Or I could continue: *At that time Western Europe
possessed no cities worthy of the name.* And you might reflect
that now we have too many of them, and they threaten to link
    up
like one horrible amorphous organism on a scale
so preposterous that everything begins to seem small, squalid,
    undistinguished—
Arches of Triumph, festal towers, canals, and churches all lost
in the general urban scrimmage. Or you might say: "But that
is ancient history, the deadest of letters. Life today is so exciting
since we are daily menaced by the prospect of extinction
in a variety of novel forms, of which ecological ones are currently
    the most popular."
So you return to your novel, written in sentences calculated
not to distress the syntax-impaired, about the adventures
of a ruthlessly ambitious yet somehow wonderful young woman,

beginning in the boondocks and ending at the headquarters
of the world's classiest perfume conglomerate, and taking in
poverty, riches, sex, irony struggle, and play, not to mention
an exhaustive kaleidoscope of despoiled but still lovely
North American landscapes along the way. And so to bed!

Yes, despite everything, isn't it good to be here
especially if, in summer, you can afford to spend your time
by some gleaming arm of the ocean with a steady supply
of cocktails at hand? Also music and X-rated videos.
Come the fall, the party circuit gets competitive, and even
the indigent can benefit, providing they have a couple of pairs
of decent shirts and pants. But I am still determined
to bend your ears, to turn your gaze back through leaf-fall
and cool breezes that bring news of the Azores or the Aleutians,
so that, reluctantly but with decision, I resort to
parallelism and human interest, the unhistorical factors:
Men shaved their beards and began to affect turbans.
Baggy pants became fashionable. Upper-class women appeared
more frequently in public, and took to giving literary soirées
in their uptown mansions. There was a craze for Islamic art,
and the erotic novel was revived for the first time in nearly a
    millennium.

But you turn up the TV reports of the latest
race- or drug-related murders, switching channels in the hope
that an accumulation of dull trivia will approximate to insight
(as if, with enough pebbles, you could build a Matterhorn),
or you are out the door on your way to a movie set in a colossal,
    painted city
that looks strangely like home, except that the colours are
    brighter, cleaner,

and the mechanism of the drawbridge is more immaculately
     Constructivist.
And you needn't worry, the hero's beautiful coat resists gunfire,
the sunset is glamorous as a billionaire's descent into bankruptcy,
a lavishly illumined liner, of archaic design, passes on the dark
     river,
and on its deck a swing band is playing close to the swimming
     pool
on which many happy couples are dancing. Ah! this is history
as we like to know it, administered by nostalgia's prefecture,
by means of which we escape the sensation that an earthquake
     has swept
all the sites of childhood away, and there is no harbour we can
     call our own!

Melancholy and fatigue
must follow any examination of the facts,
insofar as there are any that elude
the pervading glimmer of ambiguity,
our hope and curse. Today, for example, the radio warns
that the elderly and those with respiratory problems should stay
indoors, and no strenuous activity should be undertaken
lest there be faintings, seizures, infarctions, collapses—
a veritable Dance of Death on sidewalks, in gasping parks.
This announcement comes between Stravinsky's *Capriccio*
and a Schubert piano trio, and the brain divides
like a tenement full of contentious apartment dwellers. On cue,
I can't breathe. My head aches, my heart also, but I continue
to mutter as if quiet children were present who would hear me:
There were great disparities. Despite centuries of complaints
the colonnaded thoroughfare of the city was interrupted by
a quagmire into which pack animals often sank without trace.
The economic future of the state had been mortgaged to foreigners

who behaved with great arrogance, and were periodically massacred.
The plague arrived in a beautiful cloth from the East. Death
of one kind or another stared everyone in the face, but few
had the courage to return the gaze or take action. The angel
did not descend by the burnt pillar. And does not, still does not.

Fifth Spring, Sixth Autumn

I

Until I came to the island of Manhattan I always wanted to live in some other place where I could be loved or ignored as I wished, where it would seem that the great currents of the world converged—

a harbour, a city measured by rivers, metropolis and wilderness . . .

2

Yet walking past the Archive Building on a warm day in February along streets washed with light I wondered at its massive, arched structure of red brick, and I thought—not without affection—of Manchester and the changing colours of its canals, the rain drumming on the glass vaults of its exchanges and arcades.

3

From Manchester my mother writes to me: "You know, it's strange, I formed the very same opinion concerning cousin J. Last time we were in Elkstone I said to Ted, 'J is getting just like her mother.' Thank you for the postcard of the amaryllis."

4

I am taken back more than twenty years to the days in which my cousin, my sister, and I travelled—sometimes separately, sometimes together—among the Aegean archipelagoes. All three of us at once fell in love with the light, the islands, the peacock-coloured sea, but my sister also fell in love with a native of the place whom I remember as tall and wasp-waisted, like a prince of Knossos.

5

After an ill-advised solo excursion to the dismal isle of Naxos, where I lodged—unhappy as abandoned Ariadne—in a *pension* in which the rooms and all the fixtures seemed to have been designed by dwarves, I met up with them on the island of Ios, one of several disputed sites of Homer's last resting place. Dawn had just broken, illuminating a white belfry like a dovecote, and I had to find my sister. In the port a friendly priest agreed to guard my luggage while I went in search of her. I described her to people I met, and they told me where she was. So I walked over a hill and down to a beach, and into a whitewashed room where she was asleep. She awoke immediately and told me she had been dreaming of my arrival.

6

Somewhere in the weave of those days is a gay disciple of Hundertwasser, who painted vaguely *Wiener Werkstätte* designs on everybody's jeans, and an elegant Dutch heiress who had a passion for snails in garlic, and wore glass tears glued to her cheeks, and since electricity had not yet reached the place, the houses of the village glowed nearly purple in the moonlight, and at a raki-drenched party a man wearing a wing collar and no shirt played Bach on a guitar. O partitas and cassations, you still have not deserted me! And one too-hot afternoon we gathered squid that had washed up on the beach, and the ink leaked all over our hands.

7

Once, as our ferry approached the island of Seriphos, a violent squall hit. It seemed the visitation of some local god the mythologies had neglected to record. The boat heaved and lurched, and vomit streamed across the deck. We lay still as corpses as the waves crashed over us, and the salt seeped into our mouths. Then, through a narrow opening in a line of cliffs, we passed into a harbour shaped like a keyhole, and the wind died, and the bells rang all together. Then the voyage proceeded calmly under stars.

8

For a moment *we had come home*. We were a long way from Manchester's ornate, charcoal-grey façades, a long way from the narrow valleys of the Pennines, the tall chimneys of their vast and silent mills. Nor did we remember with much fondness the gardens in which we had fought and played, their orange bean-flowers and gooseberries. The world appeared to us as an immense round platform with ruins at its centre. These stark gold islands were surely the remains of some greater structure that had vanished even from legend.

9

And having reached the island of Chios, I could not afford the taxi fare from the port to the monastery of Nea Moni, where the Emperor Constantine Monomachus had ordered the creation of mosaics of a remarkable austere and hieratic cast. Nothing else like them survives from the mid-eleventh century. It is conjectured the artists must have come from the eastern provinces, but in reality we know nothing about these anonymous servants of a God to whom all art was pleasing. This is a lesson in lost causes.

10

On Lesbos, while staying in a monastery, I was offered a woman by a mustachioed man with a heavy Brooklyn accent. Later that night, stumbling into the bathroom, I found a huge bloated tomato decomposing in the stone sink. In the hills above the town there were forests of oaks entwined with bougainvillea and hibiscus. In Lefkes I entered a baroque church lighted by pretentious chandeliers, each tagged with the name of an exiled donor. At Molivos I slept on the beach where the head of Orpheus is supposed to have been borne ashore still singing. On Paros I found the grave of Archilochus, but not the marble quarries that supplied Phidias. Strangely, the bookstore in the harbour town was full of yellow-bound editions of Sade and Masoch. One volume I picked up began with an episode that concerned a priest whose particular pleasure it was to ejaculate in the faces of altar boys. On the voyage back to Piraeus my sister became desperately sick. In Athens I sold my blood to buy her a sleeper on the long train ride home, and in my agitation I confused the word that means "slowly" with the word that means "fig," which is a euphemism for "fag." These horrible people seemed to know too much about me.

I I

In the pure Euclidean space of Justinian's deconsecrated cathedral church I experienced great elation and great sadness. In the South Gallery I stood for a long time looking at the portraits of the Emperor John Comnenus and his Empress Irene—their great crowns, the striations of fatigue that marked their cheeks, and, not least, the portrait (added some years later) of their small son Alexius, who died before puberty. John, all the accounts agree, was a man of high principles, a wise and energetic ruler. Since he engaged in no spectacular massacres or obliterations of cities we know little of his personality, but the tesserae of his portrait, buried for centuries under plaster, are still brighter than any day. Wounded by a poisoned arrow while out enjoying the pleasures of the chase, he died on April 8th, 1143.

I 2

From London my sister calls to tell me of her encounter with her lover of more than twenty years ago. He had hoped to find in her consolation for his wife's infidelity and memory of his youth. She had wanted to know if passion was still possible for her. She found that it was, but that it passed quickly. She had succumbed to the love of a place, and to the figure that represented her love of the place.

13

I remember sharing a night in a deserted square in Monemvasia with a tethered goat. I remember the sound of the wind whistling through the dome of the church that crowned the ruined citadel. I remember the dawn in that place. For days I was alone and felt no need of company amid the saints, soldiers, angels, courtiers, and virgins that peopled the walls of Mistra's churches. How sad and reproachful they seemed, how elegant and human, invested with the knowledge that their "poetic cause" was soon to die.

14

I ring my cousin in Cazenovia, New York State, and she asks, "How can you stand it in the city?," and I reply, "But I love it here. Life has never been so full. Where else could I find such people and such buildings?" And I thought how the Greeks recognise only one city, though it was taken from them more than five centuries ago. They cannot forget, and in any age the exemplary city, the central city is the capital of memory.

15

And I remember how my cousin and I climbed from the black beach of Santorini up to the ancient town of Thira, and there we found a small theatre and a cluster of painted rooms lying open to the sky, perched atop a precipice, beneath which was nothing but the blue Aegean.

Streets

These glances press against you like the surges of the breeze
off the Hudson crossing Hudson Street.
What can be going on in the mind of the young,
upwardly mobile person shopping for vitamins and beansprouts
hard by *The First National Church of the Exquisite Panic?*

Doesn't the whole city cry out to him
that he must do something remarkable today?
One assumes (one can assume anything)
that behind the charming pediment of a smile
there is an interior to be explored, a suite of rooms—
a place at least big enough for a piano and a bed.

Perhaps there is only darkness, you say,
a wormeaten stair curving down from nowhere
to nothing, but that would be too bad to think of
on a day in January of such warmth it seems
a gesture of forgiveness, like the scarf
a neglected relative sent to you.

On 15th Street we assume the best, that
you will find the thing you have been looking for
in the hat shop on Greenwich Avenue,
or that winter like a curse is spent once and for all.

On 13th Street the banners blow
in sad celebration of family, friends, and lovers.
In the little triangular park by Horatio
where the homeless slept last summer
they are building a fountain from the last century.
Ah, streets where are you taking us?

Twentieth Century

Another bunch of fallen gods returning from the 8th Avenue
     gym.
The glow of their skin arouses suspicion, could be mere vanity
     and affluence.
They are perhaps creatures from another planet where nocturnes
     are never written?

But they are human under the rind—they read and work—and
     you
could look a lot more like them if you were prepared to put the
     time in,
had the stamina to withstand a crushing daily routine, and didn't
     hate

the very idea of "exercise." To what end? To what altar
of sacrifice dedicated? By all means let us return to our drinks
     and naps
and telephone conversations lest we end up looking like prime
     beef—

edible no doubt, but hardly food for thought, beyond the most
rudimentary notions and narrations: "Overcome by the heat,
the handsome electrician hastily undressed, unaware that
     soon . . ."

*

In apartments without curtains, overlooked from many angles,
masturbation is just another of anxiety's inexhaustible wellsprings,
but somehow night no longer answers my desires as once it did,

therefore let all eyelids be raised and a blind sun stand at the
     zenith.
The voyeur is not the victim of what he sees, and this is no one's
     confession:

I will continue to walk to the left and write with a nose dipped
    in paint, if I so wish—

not that I plan to do anything that would get me arrested,
but most poems, translated to a sunlit street, would be acts of
    gross indecency.
Yes, this is what I've been hiding all these years! It is *your*
    orphan,
take it in as if it had appeared by moonlight on the steps of a
    convent.

                                    *

Some hope! And do not expect anyone to be grateful
for your miraculous aperçu, though some who have followed
the slow progress of your fame may pick it up
like a laundry ticket that has slipped from your pocket

with all the momentousness of Bluebeard's seventh key.
The secret will never be revealed, since there are
no secrets. It is much too late for that. Blood
on the paving stones, blood in the throats of the flowers.

The cleaning fluid is running out. The century is coming to an
    end,
and to make it look in any way presentable or fit to live in
would be a new labour for Hercules, and yet we *have* lived in it,
and there were days we behaved rationally with nearly stoic calm,

handing out life jackets as the last comforting concept capsized,
and sometimes our clothes, our thoughts, looked elegant and
    that seemed enough:
we had added some feeble lustre to the mostly incriminating
    record.

                                    *

A decadent historicism appeared in buildings, appalling to
        purists,
and executives of telephone companies walked daily
beneath romanesque vaults and the gilded wings of statues,

then on a clouded day no one could fix in retrospect
the body became a religion, sex a kind of makeshift sacrament,
and with nothing but this dim polestar to guide us

we must now confront the idea of continual mourning
and the necessity of pain, as a friend's handsome face
is reduced to something resembling a bruised skull.

It is a time of marvels: in midsummer a wind out of nowhere
strips the trees bare; every few minutes another Marsyas is flayed,
and the same small uncomprehending dog laps at his blood.

Twentieth century, we still have much to learn from you
concerning the refinements of cruelty and its multiplication,
banal as shopping malls on the outskirts of a town,
flourishing as the centre dies and is boarded up.

Twentieth century, you are leaving us
with resurrections of dead gods who remain dead,
twitching in their galvanised graveclothes, and this is unkind,
since we have stayed faithful to you as if you were a good
        mother.

We ignored your cocaine habit and your masochism—
you appearing in the Irish bar saying, when we mentioned
your face swollen like a purple cabbage: "Oh I had a bad fall."

What kind of staircase could do that?
Tell us whose fist it was. Twentieth century, don't lie to us.
We love you and you are leaving forever.

The Ungrateful Citizens

It occurs to me that I would like to write a poem about Naples.
Perhaps I have always wanted to do this, and only realized it just
    a moment ago,
but, alas, I have never been to Naples, and yet my desire to write
    about the place
becomes more insuperable by the second. I become convinced
    that my writing desk
is on the same latitude as Naples: I have only to lean back in my
    chair,
and I incline toward the city of my dreams, and in my dreams
    my feet
rest in Manhattan while my hair rustles against the wharves of
    Naples,
and the wharves are bristling with galleons, feluccas, sloops, and
    schooners,
and how blue the sea on which they sway and jostle, how blue
    the sky
above them, except for some small clumps of cloud so white they
    are like
roses that have seen ghosts! And one could wander forever in the
    streets
that are as narrow and crooked as the wrinkles on the face of a
    wise and beautiful old woman.
Here all the shop signs are like the titles of arias by Alessandro
    Scarlatti.
The streets and squares are always busy, yet no one is ever too
    hurried:
at the slightest opportunity a man or a woman of Naples will sit
    down with you
on some weathered marble doorstep and engage you in the most
    animated conversation
concerning art or politics, your origins, their mother, the latest
    songs or scandals.

A citizen of Naples will say: "Oh, you are from Brooklyn? I have
    a cousin there.
He tells me it is a very beautiful place." He will say this out of
    pure courtesy.
In no other city have I seen so many fragrant pots of flowering
    bergamot,
or such luscious leaves of basil, or so many balconies overhung
    by noble bosoms.
In the late afternoon it is customary for the singers to leave the
    opera house,
and go about their business in full costume: here is the Orfeo of
    Monteverdi
haggling over the price of some pomegranates, and over there
    Dona Elvira
is sipping an espresso in a café while sharing a secret with a
    dishevelled Desdemona;
Don Carlos leaves a haberdashers in a fury, while Pinkerton
    enters a tobacconist's,
and Melisande (still in character) weeps beside a baroque public
    fountain
and here is Poppaea, and Dido, and Ariadne, and Judith, and
    Violetta . . .
and there goes Madame Butterfly's child eating a fruit like a
    setting sun
as he saunters down toward the waterfront. There, on the broad
    esplanade,
with its prodigious statuary, many restaurants are to be found,
and they are at once elegant and welcoming. During the heat of
    the day
their cool marble floors and gently rotating fans are a delight,
and in the evenings entire families go out to dine dressed in the
    finest clothes,

and how charming are the pink and white dresses of the young
    girls,
who resemble gardenias or oleander flowers as they settle lightly
    into their seats.
The families are very large, which is why the restaurants are so
    spacious—
stretching away into shimmering distances in which the fans stir
    the torpid fronds of palms—
and why the menus are so long and as varied as the colours of
    autumn.
Here the generations are nightly conjoined in perfect amity,
and even shy lovers may find corners in which to commune
    unnoticed
except by some musician, who wishes only to urge their love
    forward
from a tactful distance. The food, it goes without saying, is
    delicious.
In Naples the taxi drivers have, of necessity, become expert in
    the negotiation
of long flights of stairs resembling formalised cascades,
and the buses constantly circling monuments to heroes of the
    Risorgimento
seem to be dancing a siciliano as the sunlight rebounds from
    their windows
and shatters against the high walls of tenements. Beyond those
    walls, however,
in some lightless courtyard a skinny child is crying under lines of
    washing
that repeat, day after day, the same doleful sentence, and I am
    reminded
that this is the city in which songbirds were once blinded so they
    would sing

more poignantly in churches on saints' days, beating against the
    domes and the vaults . . .
and it seems that despite the cheerful beggarwomen and roguish
    merchants
bowed down by enormous, tufted turbans, despite the bravado
of virile gentlemen dressed like eighteenth-century courtesans that
    I had imagined for my Naples,
despite the numberless palaces and paintings, the extravagant
    churches, theatres,
and festivals, and the flowers that perfume even the poorest
    quarters,
it seems that all but the richest and most conservative of citizens
    cannot wait to leave my Naples.
They wish to go to the north or far to the west. They crowd the
    quays and the airport lounges,
and exhibit the horrible condition of their skin, the rags they are
    forced to wear,
the few possessions they drag behind them like so many coffins
    filled with stones.
They glare at me and say: "This is not Naples. This is a place on
    which the world has turned its back.
A cloud of lies covers it. The mansions that you saw are hovels,
    the churches tin shacks,
the parks and gardens vegetable plots and stony fields in which
    we scratch for a living.
And this is not even the site of wars and massacres, only a place
    of ordinary wretchedness.
No, we cannot be the amorous ballet the tourist requires for a
    backdrop—
O take us away, perhaps to that *island of fragrant grasses*
    mentioned in a fragment of Petronius."

Sonatinas for the New Year

1.

The clarinet enters with a mild eructation
and the other sounds merely bump around the landscape
like blindfolded children.

Let's punch a hole through it all—
the dull malingering, the crouching
on famous lawns looking for the prodigal
return of last summer's lost tennis ball.

2.

Long ago there was no way out
but out. The priest struck me on the porch,
and that was the beginning of the end of something,
confirmed when the nettles stung my legs in the avenue of trees.

3.

The peacocks screamed along the lake shore,
the storm clouds approached with gestures
like raised fists or swirling capes, and the child
slipped away to relieve himself in the bushes.

He would grow up to deny it all, except
for that moment of gathering beans in their ponderous pods
in the long rows of a field, close to the extant
foundations of medieval structures—
a central tower? a scullery? a place to sleep?

4.

Now let the small birds come and go as they please in the eaves,
and under them build a plain doorway.

It is a time for resolution, not the forced irony
of another broken pediment, or cold, cartouched tableau:
The Discovery of America: Ulysses Arrives in Maine.

5.
In a land of dupes and drugs and lipless smiles
let some things cease: no cocktail cabals,
nothing post-anything. Pull down the podium.
Silence the cameras, the mechanical cicada in the ear.

"Say howzabout a revivalist brunch for housewives,
a new Lyric Thing anyone can 'get' like the common cold?"

No wonder the penthouse-dwellers are leaving
for the south, as are their guests or ghosts or gods
in little black-and-white cars like dancing shoes.

6.
A volume of truthful epitaphs for the detested
might include: "Dead? Was he ever alive?"
or "She really hung around too long," or—

"All peoples have concurred
That had the creature here interred
Been throttled by his nurse
The world would be no worse."

But consider the scrofulous hood
that is pulled over the head of the chairman;
consider the pit that was his soul,
a loneliness like the metal teeth of a trap.

7.

The nervous radio sputtered:
"Get out before the bridge falls in the river,
before the tunnels snap like the stems of wineglasses."

We're late in starting out I know,
and the labelled suitcases remained on the stoop
for too long, coming to resemble an Italian
hill town built on terraces, but the car
was gasping on the interminable incline,
and time is like a long series of fence posts,
something we fly past at great speed in darkness.

8.

The new staircase had iced over,
but the function could not be cancelled.
The hands of the public clocks were closed in prayer,
and women's trains got caught in briars,
and stayed there shimmering like certain types of sky.
The hats resembled megaphones or Saturn's rings.

9.

The hour approached so slowly
that the minutes grew more separate,
each a gifted monomaniac confined to its cell,
recording in watercolours the light on a tree trunk,
the fuzz on a baby's head, the folds of a sleeve . . .

One might see the importance of it all
if one were not too drunk or dazed by the approach
of a giant with dead leaves and glass in his hair:
he has come merely to announce the past, out of which
your future grows like a day lily in Vermont.

10.

Or so it seems. It is the hour—
the gorgeous doom or promise of a sunset
while we remain in darkened rooms
entered by more darkness. An entire forest
and its species may be compressed into your hand,
while you take the air and walk about as the minutes allow.
It is almost nothing. It is everything. A tall figure
strolling in a park. Free for this moment.

The Drunkard in the Snow:
After Trakl

From one age to another,
The little words—the words for darkness,
Or silver, or raw meat,

The offal that is slopped into buckets
At the stark gates where women wait in winter—

From one century to another
At the queasy point of crossing

There is always the stone face of the mother
As her confinement approaches,

The white face of the sister
Like a moon drifting between cold walls—

Always the black brow of the dead town,
And jackdaws above it.

I have seen the father's shadow on the spiral stair,
I have seen him playing with the mirrors of his nightmare.

Always and always . . . .

What has happened is simple as a cube.
Autumn's cymbals clashed
At the hour of my birth. Gutters lay smashed
At the base of blackened walls. My mother's
Hand was cold. Later my sister
Made an unhappy marriage. I no longer
Heard her Schubert sonata in the next room.

O you who were punished for what you did not know,
You who confessed to everything, having nothing to confess,
You simple folk hanging by the neck from the trees,
You know it is not enough, it is never enough
To speak of the blue evenings, the drowned stairs,
And bleeding, bronze heads: they will always excel us.

The poet is always dying
Like a drunkard in the snow,
And the event is a mote in God's eye.

O my young Mathias, my nurse
And attendant (pulled from the mines
To work in the hospital) it was you who wrote:

"Always and always I think about
My dear, good captain. In the evening
He was well, and heartily told me to bring him
Coffee in the morning. But in the morning
It was different, and my captain did not need
Black coffee. Always he protected me. Sir,
I do not wish to be with these people here anymore."

World's Floor

As if we stood on some Acropolis
the view is uninterrupted for many miles,
but you must walk to one side of it, pretending
not to notice, fooling around with the underbrush,
which, come April or May, will claim
the old fireplace as its own. That's the way
it was planned, and if my dream tells me true
some few of those houses we like are still to be found,
bravely outfacing the reversals of the weather,
in Doric or in Tudor style. As to the plan

I just mentioned, it is like, but is not, a problem
of theology. We set our sights lower,
as low as the fern that sprouts in a cellar. Surely
there will be a veranda where we can smoke in summer,
blowing clouds toward the infrequent clouds above?
The issue is exile, how far we have come and will go
in a spirit of enquiry and despair . . .

Can any song be sustained?
Windows, doors, lintels, and wainscots
are all compacted into a dark ground. So also
the forests of Bohemia are denuded,
and the hawks depart. Would anger at loss
have been the correct response—
correct like a classical order that we want
either to knock down or dissolve so that
at Selinunte the temples are flowing?
(You came on the tourist bus and will soon be going.)

There is still time to travel the hills
in some fond but creaking vehicle,

and add to your definitive collection
of sleighbells and splicing pins,
but how can we go on knowing all the things we know—
that our parents were so good to us, or so bad
they were like our own maladjusted children?
Even their hairstyles were wrong . . .

Forgive everything! And at once the day
is all baskets and vases, fruit
and implausibly coloured tulips, and the mood
is ascending directly to the cool kiss of starlight,
when a dank voice out of some rank thicket
asks peremptorily: "How can you justify
your continued existence on the planet
when poetry saves no one from themselves
or their enemies?
Things you neglected in the night
have their revenge at daybreak."

I agree entirely—
I throw up my hands—
but I think for now it would be good
to stay right where we are, just sitting
or idly trawling through some forgotten
epistolary novel which begins in laughter
and ends in the most satisfying tears.
Interior improvements are always possible,
but what we see in the longing distance
could hardly be bettered, since, from where we stand,
the neighbouring state has come to resemble
a wide, pewter basin night is rapidly invading
as if a dam had broken, and no flare or glimmer

appears on its vast rim to betray the locations
of souls who must all be in there somewhere,

obdurately fixed to their names,
and the names of their desires.

The Burnt Pages

I
Cadences, confused declensions.
These are the beads of a rosary I tell in ignorance

II
History reduced to dioramas,
Technique without utility

III
The empty towns cover themselves
With a shawl of yellow grass
And whatever was once at issue here
Is no longer contested

IV
. . . And I think the metaphor,
The mere comparison, may be wrong
In the way a Homeric simile can be wrong,
Since the sea off Water Island or Point Lobos
Is not the shield of Achilles
Or anything resembling it,
Though we are, all of us, grieving
For Patroclus

V
A month since the brilliant scene
of conversation in the bar,
The promised word did not come.
Perhaps his trip had been
Extended? The world seemed dumb.
His voice on the machine
Still sounded just as keen,
But calls went unreturned.

Then from a chance encounter
In a busy street we learned
What we did not want to know:
He had gone where we could not go

VI

The clouds rest on the sidewalk,
And the city is only *a relocation of metals*.
When the sun sets there is no sound
But one imagines the sound of enormous hinges

VII

We no longer play the dances.
Our dissonances are scarcely cantabile,
And *the last kiss comes before the first*

VIII

We have washed the blood from the walls
But not from our eyes. *O my sad father*
Why were you so silent back then
Unable to think beyond tomorrow—
Each dawn a doorway
You did not want to enter

IX

The morning was clear
And I could have wished the taxi ride
From the airport longer. O, a week
Of that comfort and postponement
Would not have been too much.
I did not know what to do
When my mother opened the door.
She was a worn curtain.

She was a Trojan heroine.
The sky resembled a still lake surface.
The roses were bright but ended early.
This is the ending of the year.
Cities surround us, they shimmer
Under different names.
My mother's hair has not turned white.
The roses were bright but ended early

X

Father, don't cut down the pine.
Someone's past—not yours, not mine—
Was happy in its shadow

XI

"What is the use of it?" he asked,
"To travel to the farthest ends of the earth
To record, in the pages of a diary,
The pangs of a new nostalgia"

XII

My feet in their too-small clogs
Hurt no more than my heart
I am sad as a wooden town

XIII

My friend is a nervous man
With an unnatural fear of coffee,
With a determination to succeed
And the conviction of failure,
And only days ago three young people
Gassed themselves in a field of soybeans

XIV

Senecan morals. Summers
Hotter than the burning of Troy

XV

For long I dwelt beneath vast porticoes
And evening changed the basalt columns
Now with the approval of the great heliotropes
I piss toward dark skies very high and far

XVI

In the small square
With the weathered bleachers
The carousel of all the rancours
Turns to a desolate air
And the painted horses grow tired.
Is this all that you desired

XVII

Don't vanish, don't take the path to the river.
The child you once were floats up toward broken windows.
We remain in the shadow of the chestnut

XVIII

The meditations are numbered
One to a thousand, and they retreat
From the event like the perspectives
Of an ideal city, its streets fanning out
Into landscapes no one has bothered to imagine,
And this vast blue cave
Is only a familiar sadness

XIX

O freight trains!
Fierce winds of the plains! O
Palisades and rivers! The past
Has been lost in the dust of the road
Like the sight of a girl holding white
Cornflowers after the truck has gone by,
Entre Galveston et Mobile

XX

The leaves stir and fall back.
Now all things must be moving on
Past the moment of the poem
Which remains like an empty cast
For the limbs of a bronze hero—
An episode in the long history
Of backward glances

XXI

I remember the muscles of your side,
And the two green plants like caryatids
That framed the hotel door in Paris.
Under that dome the avowal could have been uttered,
But instead it was replaced by a figure
Meaning the infinite in Arabic, and the sentinel
Prayed for rain, encouraged by the ardour of the insects

XXII

So in the manner of a suite of dances,
Without unreasonable regret or hope,
The annual valediction unfolds with damp,
crumpled wings, and when my mother appears

In dreams, and speaks, I know I cannot answer her
Except to embrace her as if she were a ghost

XXIII
One must go on
With the echo in one's mouth.
One must go on
With a sharp ear for the fall, with an eye
For the bloodied steps on which our limbs are broken

XXIV
Book of summer we have read you,
Every word, and memorized the lines we need.
We recall the gold light on your pages. The colours turn.

The seasons are like a day stretched over a year

XXV
Father, did you forget those songs of Mahler?
The boy with a knife in his heart

XXVI
Cities surround us, burdened by their names.
Rome is a place in New York State, and Athens too,
And Carthage. Manchester is a place in Connecticut.

XXVII
The sky resembles a still lake surface.
My mother's hair has not turned white.
The roses were bright but ended early

Above the Arch

Falling asleep on the plane
I dreamt I was on a plane.
The land below was scuffed and scarred,
without trees or habitation,
bearing only the marks of what seemed to be
a retreating acid tide. It was all

very clear. We would travel
for a thousand miles before encountering
the first palisaded fort, the first town,

and each waterhole would be poisoned.
We would throw ourselves down in the mud with animals,
with starved animals whose eyes blinked
without hostility or friendship. Mirrors, jewels—

beautiful and cold,
that only said: "Leave me alone. If
I am to die here I want none of your words."

Sunlit clouds were around me
as I woke. Who before me had seen
such whiteness, so many golds and pinks
and deep blue-greys?

I observed the shadows these clouds cast on the earth.
For a moment I fell in love with a farmhouse
that seemed to exist in a valley of light
between shadows dark as bruises,

and I imagined the dusty child
who was down there in some backyard,

her small hands clutching at the strings of the kite
that had sailed up so far she became confused
and wept thinking she had lost it forever.

But she would bring it back to earth.

About the Author

JOHN ASH has won several awards for his poetry, including a Guggenheim, a Whitney, and an Ingram-Merrill. He also writes art criticism, and is currently at work on a nonfiction book about Asian Byzantium and contemporary Turkey. Born in Manchester, England, Mr. Ash lives in New York City.